Science and Technology for Children BOOKS™

Microworlds

FRANCIS HUEBER, NATIONAL MUSEUM OF NATURAL HISTORY, SMITHSONIAN INSTITUTION

W9-AWF-891

National Science Resources Center

THE NATIONAL ACADEMIES Smithsonian Institution

National Science Resources Center

The establishment of the National Science Resources Center (NSRC) by two of the nation's most prestigious institutions, the Smithsonian Institution and the National Academies, provides the United States with a unique resource for catalyzing change in science education. The NSRC is an organization of the Smithsonian Institution and the National Academies; its mission is to improve the learning and teaching of science in the nation's school districts. The NSRC disseminates information about exemplary teaching resources, develops curriculum materials, and conducts outreach programs of leadership development, technical assistance, and professional development to help school districts implement research-based science education programs for all K–12 students.

Smithsonian Institution

One of the NSRC's parent organizations is the Smithsonian Institution. The Smithsonian Institution was created by an act of Congress in 1846 "for the increase and diffusion of knowledge...." This independent federal establishment is the world's largest museum complex and is responsible for public and scholarly activities, exhibitions, and research projects nationwide and overseas. Among the objectives of the Smithsonian is the application of its unique resources to enhance elementary and secondary education.

The National Academies

The National Academies are also a parent organization of the NSRC. The National Academies are nonprofit organizations that provide independent advice to the nation on matters of science, technology, and medicine. The National Academies consist of four organizations: the National Academy of Sciences, the National Academy of Engineering, the Institute of Medicine, and the National Research Council. The National Academy of Sciences was created in 1863 by a congressional charter. Under this charter, the National Research Council was established in 1916, the National Academy of Engineering in 1964, and the Institute of Medicine in 1970.

This book is one of a series that has been designed to be an integral component of the Science and Technology for Children® curriculum, an innovative, hands-on science program for children in grades kindergarten through six. This program would not have been possible without the generous support of federal agencies, private foundations, and corporations. Supporters include the National Science Foundation, the Smithsonian Institution, the U.S. Department of Defense, the U.S. Department of Education, the John D. and Catherine T. MacArthur Foundation, the Dow Chemical Company Foundation, the Amoco Foundation, Inc., DuPont, the Hewlett-Packard Company, the Smithsonian Institution Educational Outreach Fund, and the Smithsonian Women's Committee.

Acknowledgments

Microworlds is part of a series of books for students in kindergarten through sixth grade, and it is an integral part of the Science and Technology for Children® (STC®) curriculum program. The purpose of these books is to enhance and extend STC's inquiry-based investigations through reading. Research has shown that students improve their reading skills when challenged with interesting and engaging reading materials. In the process, key science concepts that students have been learning can be reinforced. The Teacher's Guide that accompanies the STC program gives some information on how to integrate this book with the program's inquiry-centered investigations. Those students interested in reading these books on their own will find them easy to read as stand-alone texts. All students will especially enjoy reading about highlights of the Smithsonian Institution's varied and unique museums.

The book has undergone rigorous review by experts in the field to ensure that all the information is current and accurate. A nationally recognized reading specialist has worked with us to create stories that are at a reading level that is appropriate for students in fourth and fifth grades. We have also varied the reading level throughout the book so that all students—no matter what their reading proficiency—can find stories that are both interesting and challenging.

The NSRC greatly appreciates the efforts of all the individuals listed below. Each contributed his or her expertise to ensure that the book is of the highest quality.

Science and Technology for Children Books: *Microworlds*

National Science Resources Center Staff and Consultants

Sally Goetz Shuler
Executive Director

Marilyn Fenichel
Managing Editor (consultant)

Linda Harteker
Senior Editor (consultant)

Heather Dittbrenner
Copy Editor (consultant)

Gail Peck
Designer (consultant)

Heidi M. Kupke
Graphic Designer

Max-Karl Winkler
Illustrator

John Norton
Assistant Illustrator (consultant)

Christine Hauser
Photo Editor

Susan Tannahill
Webmaster and Database Specialist

Kimberly Wayman
Procurement and Financial Assistant

Research and Development Staff and Advisors

David Marsland
Co-Director, Professional Development Center
NSRC

Henry Milne
Co-Director, Professional Development Center
NSRC

Carla Dove
Museum Specialist
Department of Vertebrate Zoology
National Museum of Natural History
Smithsonian Institution
Washington, DC

Bill Dimichele
Curator
Department of Invertebrate Zoology
National Museum of Natural History
Smithsonian Institution
Washington, DC

Marcy Heacker
Museum Specialist
Department of Vertebrate Zoology
National Museum of Natural History
Smithsonian Institution
Washington, DC

Duane W. Hope
Research Zoologist
Department of Invertebrate Zoology
National Museum of Natural History
Smithsonian Institution
Washington, DC

Craig Laufer
Associate Professor of Biology
Hood College
Frederick, MD

Linda H. Mosely, MD
Orthopedic Surgeon
Alexandria, VA

Beth B. Norden
Museum Specialist
Department of Invertebrate Zoology
National Museum of Natural History
Smithsonian Institution
Washington, DC

Scott Whittaker
Laboratories of Analytical Biology
National Museum of Natural History
Smithsonian Institution
Washington, DC

Annemarie Sullivan Palincsar
Jean and Charles Walgreen Professor of Reading and Literacy
School of Education
University of Michigan
Ann Arbor, MI

Ian MacGregor
President
Science Education Associates
Berkeley, CA

Judith White
Curriculum Developer
STC Discovery Decks
Berkeley, CA

Carolina Biological Supply Company Staff

Dianne Gerlach
Director of Product Development

David Heller
Department Head, Product Development

Robert Mize
Department Head, Publications

Jennifer Manske
Publications Manager

Gary Metheny
Editor

Cindy Morgan
Senior Curriculum Product Manager

Science and Technology for Children BOOKS™

Microworlds

CONTENTS

p. 12

p. 18

p. 58

p. 60

ABOVE—PHOTO CREDITS: (FROM TOP): © 2003, SMITHSONIAN INSTITUTION, JAMES DI LORETO; COURTESY OF BETH B. NORDEN; SMITHSONIAN INSTITUTION, JAMES DI LORETO; CARLA DOVE AND MARCY HEACKER, NATIONAL MUSEUM OF NATURAL HISTORY, SMITHSONIAN INSTITUTION

COVER—PHOTO CREDITS: (FROM TOP LEFT, CLOCKWISE): COURTESY OF CAROLINA BIOLOGICAL SUPPLY COMPANY; NATIONAL MUSEUM OF HEALTH AND MEDICINE; COURTESY OF DAVID MARSLAND

Introduction

There is more to the world than meets the eye. Our eyes cannot see the tiny organisms, or microorganisms, that live just about everywhere—in the soil, in ponds and lakes, and even on and in our own bodies. We know about these microorganisms because of a tool invented in the 1500s—the microscope.

Microscopes made people aware of a world that they didn't know existed. Microscopes made apparent that which had been invisible to us. Suddenly, there was so much more to learn.

This book, *Microworlds*, is about the tool that opened up this invisible world to humans and some important discoveries that have emerged as a result.

PART 1 explores how the microscope was invented, and how the technology continues to improve. Now that people can see the world with new eyes, they can solve interesting scientific mysteries. For example, microscopes have enabled scientists to better understand what happened in the city of Pompeii the day Mt. Vesuvius erupted hundreds of years ago, even though there are few records of what happened. Microscopes can also be used to answer everyday questions, such as which kind of bee pollinates cantaloupes. These intriguing stories and the problems they address are vivid examples of the importance of studying microorganisms. After reading these stories, you may become excited about microscopes. If so, you can read the last story in the section for instructions on how to make your own microscope.

PART 2 shows what microorganisms—from bacteria to worms—look like up close. Images taken with a sophisticated type of microscope called a scanning electron microscope, or SEM, make this possible. And have you ever seen pink flamingos at the zoo? You probably thought that they were born that color. But microorganisms play a big role in making pink flamingos pink. You'll have to read the story to find out what that role is.

THE STORIES IN PART 3 explore how microorganisms affect our lives. They can be both helpful and harmful. For example, some microorganisms can be used to create vaccines, which protect people from serious diseases. Others work to create popular foods, such as yogurt and pickles. On the other hand, some microorganisms can be harmful. They can cause serious illnesses, such as strep throat.

While you cannot see microorganisms without a microscope, you should be aware that they are all around you. The next time you brush your teeth, think about the bacteria that are lurking in your mouth. When you take a walk outside, take a minute to think about the microorganisms living in the soil. Microorganisms are everywhere, an important part of our world.

 If you see this icon in the upper right-hand corner, it's a story about scientists and the work they do.

PART 1

Seeing the World with New Eyes

The stories in this section include the following:

- Microscopes—Enlarging Our World
- Operating a High-Powered Microscope
- Mysteries of Pompeii
- Turning the Microscope on Bees
- Surgery Through a Lens
- Matchbox Microscope

These stories introduce you to microscopes, the tool that opened up a new world. Read about how the first microscopes were invented and how a series of inventors improved them. Find out the latest in microscope technology and discover how this amazing tool is used to solve intriguing problems. In addition, learn how microscopes can be used during operations.

If you would like to see this new world for yourself by using your own microscope, you will find instructions on how to make a microscope.

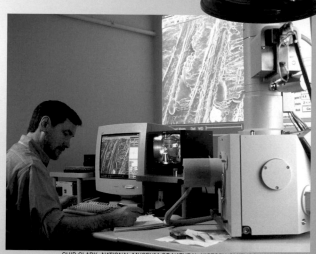

NATIONAL MUSEUM OF HEALTH AND MEDICINE

CHIP CLARK, NATIONAL MUSEUM OF NATURAL HISTORY, SMITHSONIAN INSTITUTION

Are there any similarities between these two kinds of microscopes? If you can't answer this question now, you'll be able to once you finish reading about them.

Microscopes

ENLARGING Our World

DO YOU WEAR GLASSES? If so, you know that some lenses can make things look clearer. People have worn eyeglasses, which were once called "spectacles," since the end of the 13th century.

Eyeglasses improve our vision, but they still don't allow us to see objects that are very, very small. That takes another important invention—the microscope.

The first microscopes were much like magnifying lenses. People put an object on a metal plate, or stage, and looked at it through a lens. These devices could make things look up to 10 times bigger than they actually were. People used them to look at fleas and other tiny insects. For this reason, they were called "flea glasses." Flea glasses were fun to experiment with, but they weren't thought of as scientific tools.

NATIONAL MUSEUM OF HEALTH AND MEDICINE

People liked to look through flea glasses. But they didn't know they were doing science. They thought they were just having fun.

The Janssens invented a compound microscope that Robert Hooke perfected.

A Team of Inventors

Two inventors, a father-and-son team, soon came along to change all that. They lived in Holland, and their names were Hans and Zacharias Janssen. The Janssens were eyeglass makers, so they knew a lot about lenses and magnification. What they invented was a big step forward from the flea glass. ▶

They invented the first microscope that used more than one lens. This tool is called a compound microscope. In about 1595, they put several lenses in a narrow tube. When they looked at a small object through the tube, it appeared greatly enlarged.

BILLINGS MICROSCOPE COLLECTION, NATIONAL MUSEUM OF HEALTH AND MEDICINE, ARMED FORCES INSTITUTE OF PATHOLOGY

Leeuwenhoek's microscope sitting on a display stand

Many consider the Janssens' invention to be the first true compound microscope. "Micro" means small, and "scope" means to see. This tool enabled people to see very small objects.

Microscopes Get Better and Better

By the middle of the 1600s, microscopes had improved even more. At least two other inventors contributed to these changes. The first was Anton van Leeuwenhoek.

Leeuwenhoek also lived in Holland. While working in a fabric store, he used magnifying glasses to count the number of threads in pieces of cloth. He wondered whether the lenses could be improved. Eventually, he discovered new ways of grinding and polishing lenses. By grinding, he made the lenses smaller and more curved.

Leeuwenhoek's microscopes had only one lens. However, they could magnify objects more than 270 times. The reason was his new and improved lens.

Leeuwenhoek used his microscope to learn about the natural world. He was one of the first scientists to observe and draw tiny living creatures in a sample of water. Leeuwenhoek also looked at blood under his microscope. He was able to see that blood contained tiny red discs— what we now know to be red blood cells. In addition, he is thought to be the first person to see bacteria, draw what they look like, and publish those drawings.

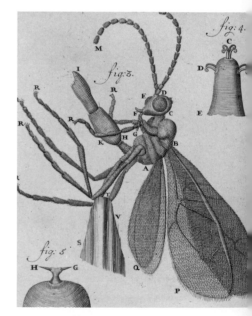

Leeuwenhoek had a major problem with his microscopes. They needed a lot of light. To view objects, he had to stand in a doorway and hold his microscope in the direct sunlight.

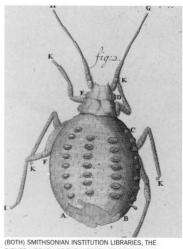

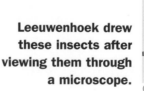

Leeuwenhoek drew these insects after viewing them through a microscope.

(BOTH) SMITHSONIAN INSTITUTION LIBRARIES, THE DIBNER LIBRARY OF THE HISTORY OF SCIENCE AND TECHNOLOGY

Robert Hooke's Contribution

Robert Hooke, a famous English scientist and inventor, solved the light problem for his microscope by putting a mirror at the microscope's base. The mirror reflected light onto the object. That way, Hooke didn't have to stand in the sunlight to see microorganisms. Instead, he could use his mirror to direct the light to the microscope's stage.

With his compound microscope, Hooke could see flies and other small creatures magnified. The drawing shown below was done by Hooke himself. It shows a fly magnified about 30 times.

The microscope opened up a whole new world. For the first time, scientists could see microorganisms—creatures too small to see with the eyes alone—and greater detail in small organisms and objects.

In this book, you will read about many of the things that scientists have discovered with this wonderful tool and how this new knowledge has helped change the world. ■

LENS

An early microscope with two lenses and a mirror

LENS

MIRROR

NATIONAL MUSEUM OF HEALTH AND MEDICINE

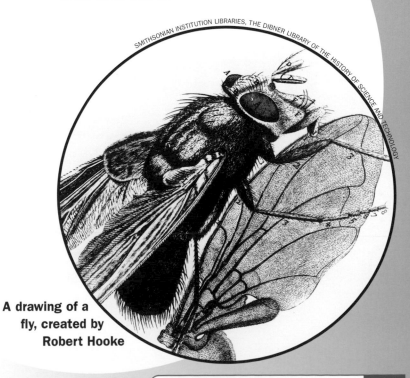

SMITHSONIAN INSTITUTION LIBRARIES, THE DIBNER LIBRARY OF THE HISTORY OF SCIENCE AND TECHNOLOGY

A drawing of a fly, created by Robert Hooke

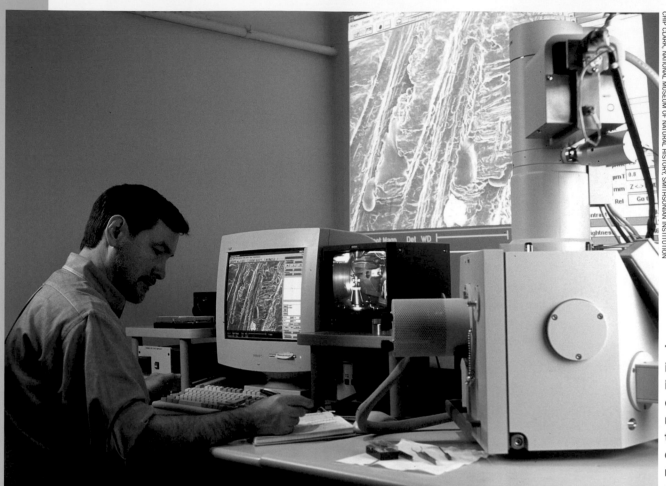

CHIP CLARK, NATIONAL MUSEUM OF NATURAL HISTORY, SMITHSONIAN INSTITUTION

This scientist is viewing an image on his computer monitor from the scanning electron microscope on his right.

Operating a High-Powered Microscope

MICROSCOPES HAVE COME A LONG WAY SINCE THE DAYS OF LEEUWENHOEK AND HOOKE. Today, some microscopes look a lot like computers. These microscopes are called scanning electron microscopes, or SEMs for short.

Three of these modern microscopes fill a large lab at the Smithsonian Institution's National Museum of Natural History in Washington, D.C. Scott Whittaker manages the lab and helps the museum scientists use these microscopes.

© 2003, SMITHSONIAN INSTITUTION, JAMES DI LORETO

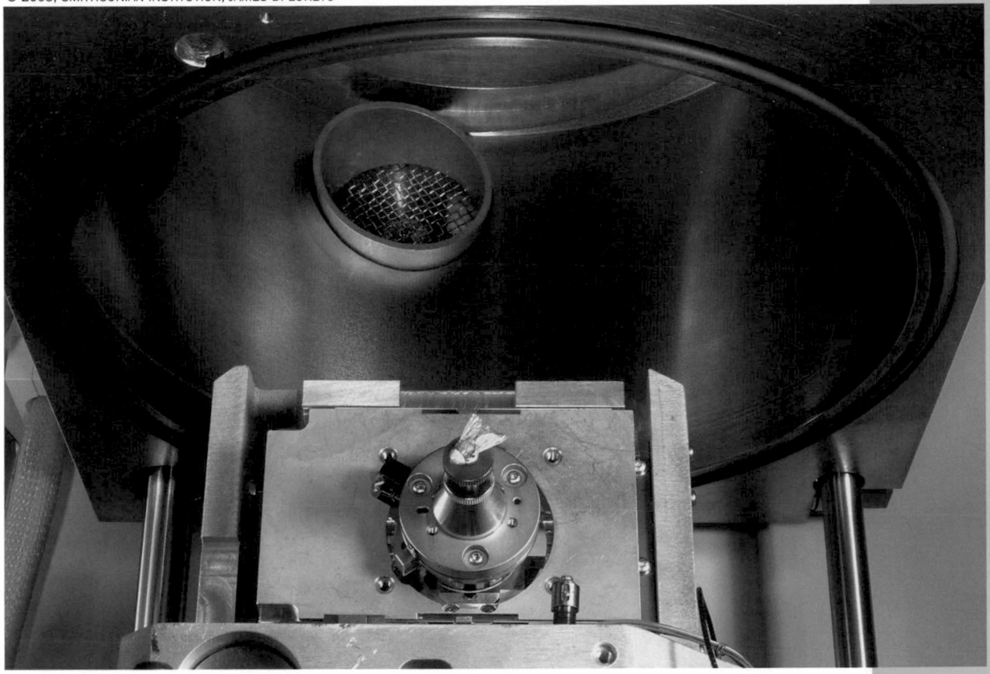

The specimen chamber, shown here, is where objects to be viewed are placed. Electrons are scanned across objects in this chamber.

"I became interested in electron microscopes because they can show the structure and possibly the function of life's processes all the way down to the most basic level at any given point in time," says Scott. "And almost anyone who can play video games or surf the Web on a computer can operate a modern SEM."

Using an SEM

How do SEMs work? First, you don't look through an eyepiece, like you do with a light microscope. Instead, you see the image on a computer screen. Second, SEMs don't use light to look at an object. They use a beam of electrons. Electrons are one of three types of particles that make up atoms. The object to be studied is put into a special chamber. All the air is pumped out, creating a vacuum. An electron beam is scanned across the surface of the object in the SEM chamber. The results of this scanning process are sent to a computer and displayed on a monitor.

Getting an Organism Ready for an SEM

Preparing a small organism, such as an insect, for viewing through an SEM is a very unusual process. First, the insect is killed and dried in a special way to prevent it from shriveling, or curling up. Then it is mounted on a holder, or stub, that fits in the microscope. It is then coated with a thin coat of gold. This is done so that its surface can conduct electricity and react to the electron beam. A technician then places the specimen into the specimen chamber. The insect is now ready for viewing. ▸

Showing the object on a screen this large makes a tiny creature larger than life.

When the image appears on the computer screen, researchers can print a copy of the image. They can also save it as a file or transmit it electronically to other scientists.

To the right are two images taken through an SEM. The top image is a scale bug eating a garden ivy root. The bottom image is of insects feeding on milkweed. They almost look like creatures from a science fiction movie.

The SEM is an amazing technology. It really does give us a chance to view the world in a new way. ■

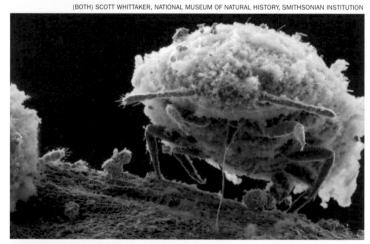

A scalebug eating a garden ivy root

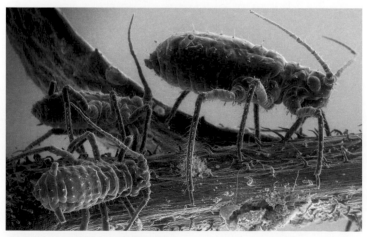

Aphids feeding on milkweed

Mysteries of POMPEII

Almost 2,000 years ago, the Italian town of Pompeii was a prosperous place. About 20,000 people lived there. Rich citizens from the city of Rome built summer homes in this lovely city.

Pompeii lay in the shadow of Mt. Vesuvius. Farmers grew grapes in the rich soil at the foot of the mountain. Mt. Vesuvius was a volcano, but it hadn't erupted for 800 years. People thought they had no reason to fear it.

They were wrong. On August 24 of the year 79 AD, Mt. Vesuvius erupted ferociously. Pompeii was buried by more than 6 meters (20 feet) of stone, lava, and volcanic ash.

SEM Offers Clues

In the 18th century, archaeologists, scientists who study remains from past cultures, began excavations at Pompeii. They found a city frozen in time. The hot ash preserved life as it was at the moment of the eruption.

The explorations continued for decades. As time passed, scientists could use more powerful tools for their investigations of Pompeii. One of them was the scanning electron microscope (SEM). These photos show some of the objects found in the ruins. ▸

(ALL) FRANCIS HUEBER, NATIONAL MUSEUM OF NATURAL HISTORY, SMITHSONIAN INSTITUTION

Clover flower magnified 28 times

Scavenger beetle magnified 120 times

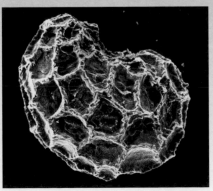

Poppy seed magnified 100 times

Alfalfa seed pod magnified 18 times

Other material that archaeologists found looked like shiny, black glass. It was brittle and broke easily.

As the scientists inspected the black material more closely, probably with a hand lens, they discovered it was plant and animal material that had turned to carbon. After viewing the carbonized material under the SEM, scientists made a final determination. They identified more than 80 different plants—olive leaves, grapevines, fern leaves, and many weeds and wildflowers. These plants still grow in Italy today.

A Way of Life Revealed

There are many possible explanations for what was happening the day the volcano erupted.

This image shows a cross-section of a grapevine, which has been magnified 66 times.

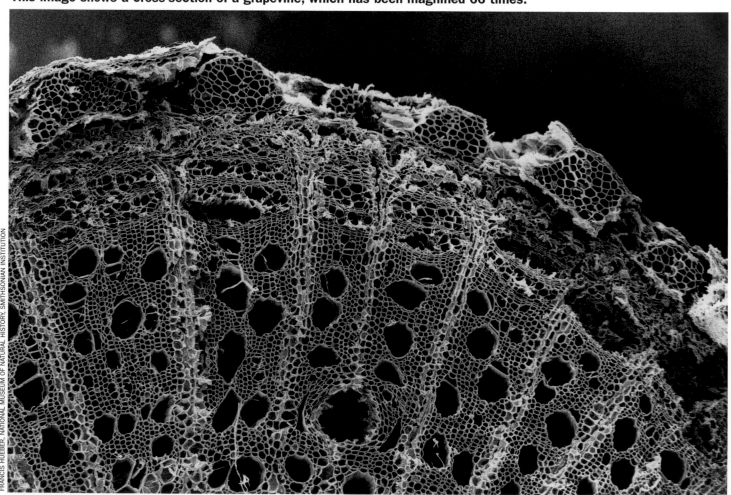

Perhaps a few days before Vesuvius erupted, the caretaker had trimmed his grapevines and cleared away the weeds and flowers growing nearby. He may have brought the trimmings inside to store. Maybe he was going to use them as mulch or as food for his cows or goats. Then the volcano erupted. Pompeii disappeared.

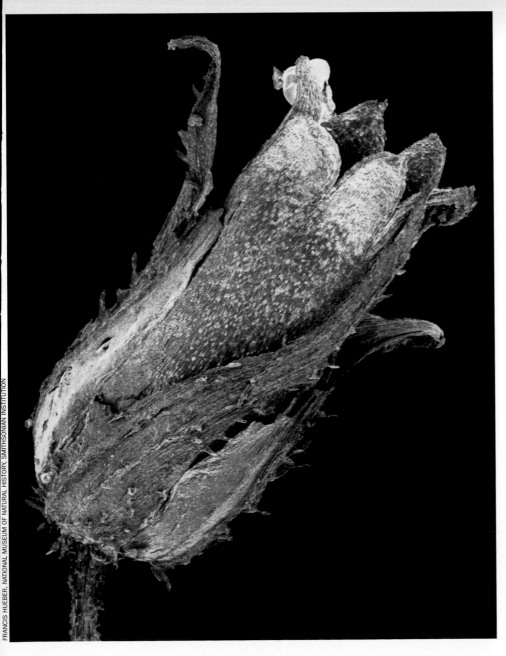

Chickweed seed pod
magnified 50 times

Today, Pompeii gives scientists a chance to see evidence of life as it was nearly 2,000 years ago. And thanks to tools such as the SEM, scientists can uncover clues about what life was like in Pompeii many years ago. ■

Turning the Microscope on Bees

Many farmers on Maryland's Eastern Shore grow cantaloupe plants. They know that the blossoms of these plants have to be pollinated in order to produce fruit. The farmers also know that insects—usually bees—take care of the pollinating job very well. Bees pick up and brush off pollen as they move from blossom to blossom.

A few years ago, the farmers decided that they wanted to harvest more cantaloupes. But they didn't want to plant more seeds. Instead, they wanted each plant to produce more fruit. They assumed that honeybees were the best pollinators. So they decided to boost the number of bees. They rented hives of honeybees and placed them in the fields.

Farmers placed beehives like this one in their cantaloupe fields.

Researcher in the Cantaloupe Fields

Beth Norden, a scientist from the Smithsonian Institution's National Museum of Natural History, went to the cantaloupe farms. She was studying pollination. As Beth observed the insects around the melon plants, she had a surprise. The honeybees seemed to be avoiding the cantaloupe blossoms! They seemed to prefer the larger squash and watermelon blossoms in nearby fields.

Beth also noticed some smaller bees flying under the leaves of the cantaloupe flowers. She knew that these were small carpenter bees. These bees are smaller than their relatives—the large carpenter bees—and nest in twigs.

Beth thought, "Perhaps these small carpenter bees, not the honeybees, are doing most of the cantaloupe pollinating."

Collecting Evidence

She decided to check out her hunch. She knew that each type of plant has its own kind of pollen. Each kind of pollen looks different. She would use a scanning electron microscope (SEM) to look at the bees and the pollen they carried. She would try to find out what kind of pollen each type of bee was carrying.

Beth collected pollen samples from the blossoms of squash and watermelon plants, as well as from the cantaloupe plants in the farmers' fields. Then she collected some carpenter bees and some honeybees. She took the samples to her lab and prepared them.

The photos below and one on the top left of the next page show pollen that Beth collected from three kinds of blossoms. The cantaloupe pollen (top) is smooth and shaped something like a pyramid. The watermelon pollen (bottom) is round and full of holes. ▸

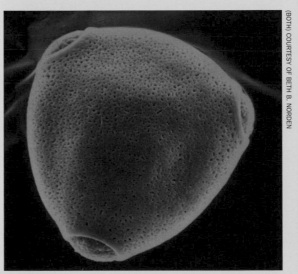

(BOTH) COURTESY OF BETH B. NORDEN

Cantaloupe pollen magnified thousands of times

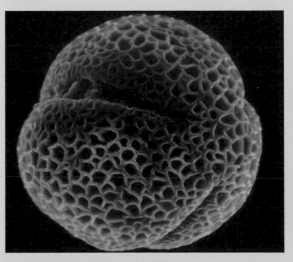

Watermelon pollen magnified thousands of times

And this is squash pollen. It is round and has lots of spines.

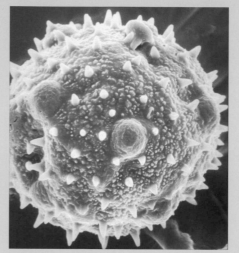

Squash pollen magnified hundreds of times

Zooming In ...
on the Small Carpenter Bee

Beth put a small carpenter bee in the SEM. Can you see pollen grains around the base of the antenna in the image below at left?

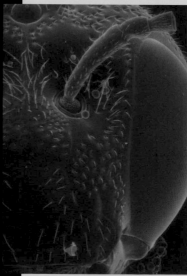

The head of the small carpenter bee has been magnified 72 times.

(ALL) COURTESY OF BETH B. NORDEN

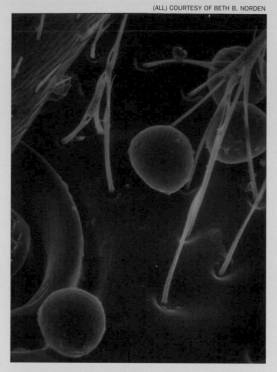

The small carpenter bee's head has been magnified hundreds of times more in this picture than in the one below left. It looks very different now, doesn't it?

IN THE PICTURE ABOVE, the small carpenter bee's head has been magnified 440 times. Now Beth could identify the pollen.

Zooming In...on the Honeybee

Beth's next step was to look at the honeybee in the SEM. The honeybee, shown below at right, has been magnified so much that Beth could see pollen here, too—but was it cantaloupe pollen?

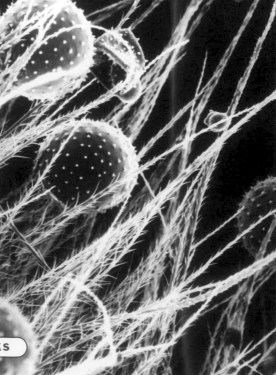

What do you think? Which kind of bee was most likely pollinating the cantaloupes?

Which Bee Was Doing the Work?

To confirm her suspicions, Beth examined other honeybees and carpenter bees that she brought to the lab. Both the small carpenter bees and the honeybees had lots of pollen on their bodies. But the honeybees had very little cantaloupe pollen. Beth confirmed her hypothesis: When it comes to cantaloupes, the small carpenter bees do most of the work.

COURTESY OF BETH B. NORDEN

Honeybees may find it difficult to get into the small cantaloupe flowers, while small carpenter bees have no trouble.

Beth had additional observations to support her findings. She observed honeybees heading toward the larger blossoms of the squash and watermelon plants. Honeybees also are much larger than the carpenter bees. Beth speculated on why the two types of bees prefer different plants. She thought that the larger honeybees find it hard to get into the small cantaloupe blossoms. The cantaloupe flowers are harder to find because they are hidden beneath the cantaloupe leaves. What's more, the cantaloupe blossoms produce less nectar than the larger blossoms do.

Beth concluded that the honeybees head for the larger nectar supply found in big blossoms. The carpenter bees get what they need from the cantaloupe blossoms. The blossoms, although small, provide them with plenty of food.

So the small carpenter bees pollinate the cantaloupes. Each bee is adapted to collecting nectar from different types of flowers. This way, they do not compete for the same source of food.

Thanks to Beth's research, the farmers learned a lesson in pollination. Bees, like many forms of life, are specialists. Whether large or small, they find food sources that are most appropriate for them.

Now the farmers know why their experiment didn't work. They brought in the wrong kind of bee. It's those small carpenter bees that could help produce more cantaloupes. Next time, the farmers should try those and see what happens. ■

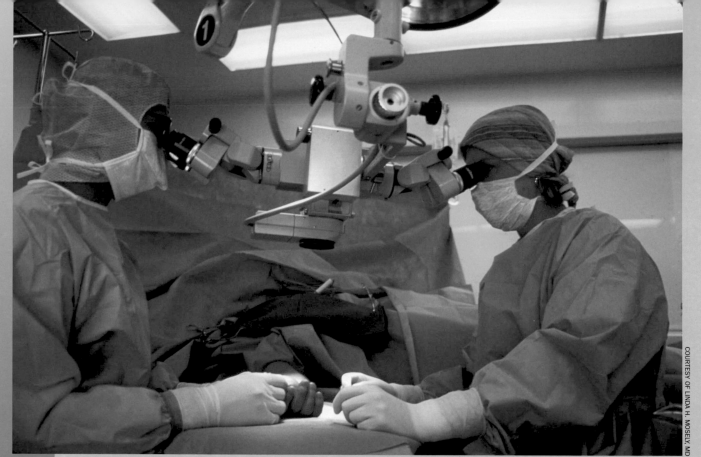

**Dr. Linda Mosely
and her assistant perform
a delicate operation.**

Surgery
Through a Lens

WHAT'S GOING ON HERE? Yes, it's an operation, but it's surgery of a "micro"
kind. Surgeon Linda Mosely is performing the operation while looking
through a special microscope. It is called a dual stereo microscope. This
microscope has two sets of eyepieces. Two people can look through it at the
same time. It is "stereo" because it can reveal a different angle to each eye.
This provides the clearest possible image during the operation.

　While her hands are busy performing the operation, Dr. Mosely focuses and
moves the microscope with a foot pedal. Dr. Mosely and her colleague are using
this microscope to get the best possible view of an injured finger. In the image
above, the two surgeons are repairing a nerve in a patient's hand. Without this
microscope, the surgeons would not be able to complete the operation.

"Micro" Instruments

To do this job, Dr. Mosely needs the right tools—micro-instruments. These are similar to the tools used by other surgeons, but they are much smaller.

One of the surgeon's tasks is to sew tissue. This requires a needle and thread. The photo directly below shows the micro-needle and thread that Dr. Mosely uses during these operations. To hold these tiny instruments, Dr. Mosely uses an extra-small needle holder.

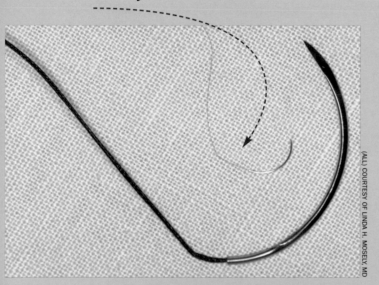

(ALL) COURTESY OF LINDA H. MOSELY, MD

Do you see where the arrow is pointing? That's the delicate thread used in microsurgery. You can also see the needle, shaped like a hook on the end.

Follow the Operation: Take a Closer Look

Dr. Mosely is ready to repair the nerve in the patient's hand, which was damaged when it was caught in a door.

1. The patient's hand is being prepared for the operation. The dark, wavy line on the finger indicates where Dr. Mosely will cut. ▶

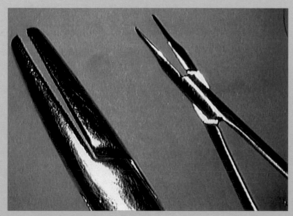

The needle holder (above right) used in microsurgery is much smaller than the one used in general surgery (above left).

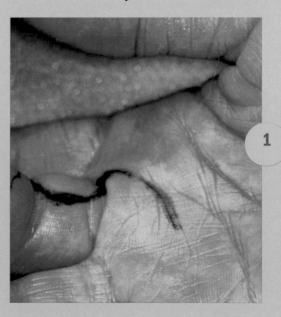

1

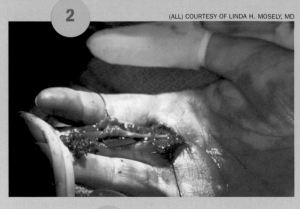

2. Dr. Mosely cuts open the finger. As she expected, the nerve is covered with scar tissue. The scar tissue was formed after the finger was injured. Because of the scar tissue, the patient has not been able to straighten her finger since she got the injury.

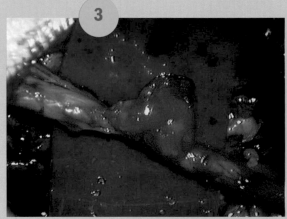

3. Here's what the nerve looks like under the microscope. The lump is the scar tissue.

4. Dr. Mosely removes the scar tissue. Within weeks, the patient will regain full use of her hand.

A New Way of Working

Trained in general plastic surgery, Dr. Mosely says it took time to get used to operating while looking through a microscope.

"It's important to be very steady and to concentrate extra hard while doing microsurgery," Dr. Mosely continues. "Movements are greatly exaggerated at this level, so a tiny twitch can end up as a big mistake." To make her hands as steady as possible, Dr. Mosely often props her arms on pillows. She never drinks coffee or other beverages that contain caffeine before an operation.

Operating while looking through a scope is "like being in a new environment," says Dr. Mosely. But it is an environment that has enabled Dr. Mosely to fix the smallest possible injury. ■

Matchbox Microscope

Although today's commercial microscopes are very sophisticated, people can still make basic micro-scopes for their own use. These microscopes may not magnify objects a lot, but they do let you see a little more than you can see with your eyes alone.

Follow these directions to make a microscope out of two matchboxes and a drop of water.

Use These Materials

- 1 sheet of tracing paper
- 1 pencil
- 1 index card
- 2 small empty matchboxes
- 1 small rubber band
- Scissors
- 1 cup of water
- Petroleum jelly

You can make a lens holder from this outline. The steps on the next page will tell you how.

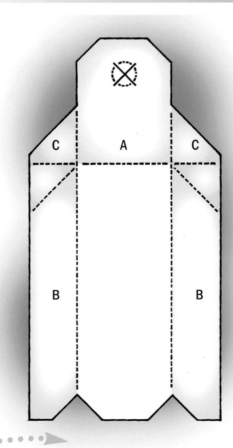

The Lens Holder

FIRST, make the lens holder. Here's how.

1. Trace the outline of the lens holder, shown on the previous page, on tracing paper. Then cut along the outline.

The first step is easy!

2. Lay your tracing paper outline on an index card and draw around the outline. Cut along this outline. This is your lens holder.

You're making progress now.

3. Draw dotted lines and an X on your lens holder. You can see the X clearly on the drawing on page 23. Use a pencil point to punch a hole where the X is.

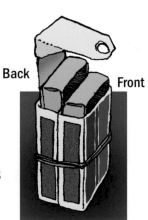

4. Fold your lens holder as shown in the figure. First, fold "A" down on the dotted lines.

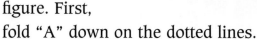

FOLD "B" (THE WINGS) UP. Continue folding until the edges of the wings meet.

CONTINUE FOLDING "B" UNTIL THE EDGES ARE FLAT.

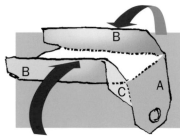

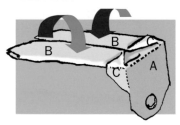

In the process, "C" becomes a triangular support for "A." You've just made a lens holder.

The Microscope

Now you're ready to make the microscope.

1. Join the lens holder and matchboxes. Slide your lens holder under the drawer of one of the matchboxes. Lay the second matchbox on top of the first one, with the open drawer facing out. Put a rubber band around both matchboxes. Stand the matchboxes up.

Now the frame of the microscope is done.

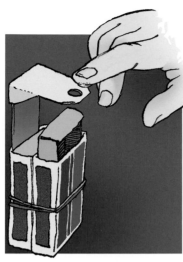

Making the lens is an important part of building your own microscope.

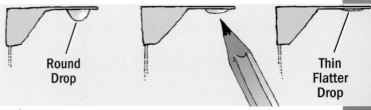

Round Drop

Thin Flatter Drop

These pictures show how to change the shape of the lens.

2. Make the lens. To do this, put a small amount of petroleum jelly on your finger and rub it around the edges of the hole on both sides. Wipe off any globs of petroleum jelly.

Dip one finger into a cup of water. Use your finger to move the drop of water to the hole. The water drop will slide into the hole and hang there. It may take several tries to get this right. If the drop falls off, put some more petroleum jelly around the hole and try again.

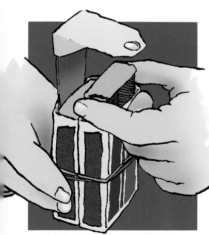

Focus the magnifier by moving the stage.

3. See if your microscope works. Put a small object on the drawer of the microscope. This part is the stage of your microscope. Look at the object through the water drop. Focus your magnifier by moving the stage—with the object on it—up or down. Find the right height at which each object is in focus.

4. Change the lens. You can change the shape of the lens and the way it magnifies by adding or taking away water. Here's how:

■ To make your lens rounder, add more water. You can do that by dipping your finger in the water cup again and gently touching the top of the lens.

■ To make your lens flatter, take away water. Use the tip of a pencil to brush away a little bit. How does changing the shape of the lens change the way the object appears?

Find some objects to look at under the microscope. A paper towel, a leaf, or a piece of cork work well. How do objects look when the drop is round? How do they look when the drop is flatter?

With your microscope, you can see the world through new lenses. ■

Seeing the World with New Eyes

THAT'S A FACT!　Instead of using light to see objects, SEMs use a beam of electrons.

THAT'S EASY!　What was Robert Hooke's contribution to the development of microscope technology?

WHAT DO YOU THINK?　Now that you've read the stories in Part 1, do you think there are any similarities between early microscopes and SEMs? Support your ideas with evidence from the stories.

I KNOW THAT!　How did the SEM enable scientists to solve problems? Use examples from the stories in this section.

PART 2

Microorganisms Up Close

You have seen how microscopes have changed our ideas about the world. Now journey into the world of microorganisms and see what they really look like and how they behave. They are much more complex than you may have imagined.

In this section, you will read the following stories:

- *Volvox*
- Vinegar Eelworm
- It's a Wormy World
- Smile and Meet Some Bacteria
- You Are What You Eat

In each of these stories, you will see different microorganisms up-close and personal. They come in different shapes and are adapted to their environment in many

DAWN ADIN, DEPARTMENT OF MICROBIOLOGY, UNIVERSITY OF GEORGIA, ATHENS

DUANE HOPE, NATIONAL MUSEUM OF NATURAL HISTORY, SMITHSONIAN INSTITUTION

You will be reading about these two organisms in this section. As you read, think about how they move, what they eat, and other characteristics that make each one unique.

ways. They are all species of organisms that have lived on Earth for a long time. After reading these stories, you will have a deeper understanding of the world around you.

Volvox

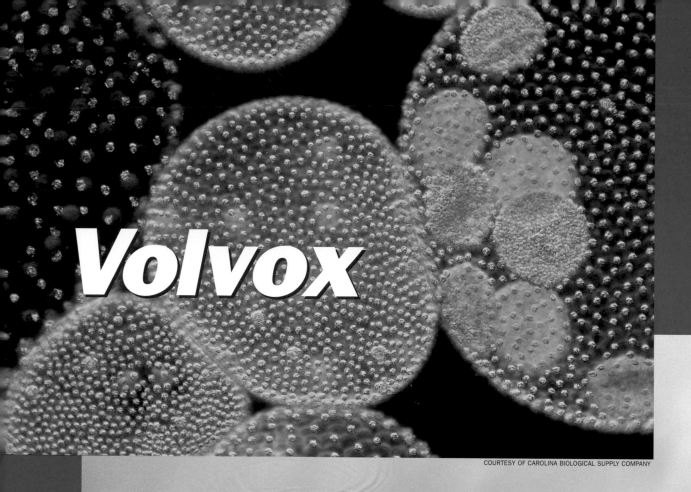

WHY DO YOU THINK THERE IS OFTEN A GREENISH FILM ON THE SURFACE OF A POND? CHANCES ARE, THE FILM IS A GREAT NUMBER OF TINY ORGANISMS CALLED ALGAE. ALTHOUGH ALGAE LOOK LIKE PLANTS, THEY ACTUALLY BELONG TO A GROUP OF ORGANISMS CALLED PROTISTS. PROTISTS VARY A GREAT DEAL, BUT THEY ALL TEND TO LIVE IN MOIST PLACES.

ALTHOUGH ALGAE ARE NOT PLANTS, THEY HAVE SOME OF THE SAME FEATURES AS PLANTS. MOST ALGAE CONTAIN A SUBSTANCE CALLED CHLOROPHYLL. CHLOROPHYLL GIVES ALGAE THEIR GREEN COLOR.

There are more than 20,000 different species of algae. One kind of alga that is particularly beautiful and interesting is called *Volvox*. Each *Volvox* is made up of one cell—the smallest organized unit of life. *Volvox* cells cannot be seen without a microscope.

Volvox live together in large groups called colonies. A colony may contain as many as 50,000 cells. They stay together by clinging to a clear, jellylike substance shaped like a ball.

Each *Volvox* cell has two flagella. Flagella are whiplike structures that the cells use to move. In a *Volvox* colony, all the cells' flagella move together. They propel the colony around in the water. The *Volvox* colony needs to move to get into the sunlight. Like all algae, *Volvox* make their own food, and the process requires sunlight.

The Life Cycle of *Volvox*

Like all organisms, *Volvox* goes through a life cycle. **PHOTO 1** shows a young Volvox colony that is just starting to grow. Each tiny circle is a cell. The *Volvox* colony in **PHOTO 2** has just emerged from the parent colony. Some of its cells are larger than the others. The large cells are the reproductive cells. These cells are called gonidia. They divide to form a new generation of *Volvox*.

Two days after the *Volvox* colony emerges from its parent colony, the colony is much bigger. The amount of clear, jelly-like material between the cells has increased. The cells have grown larger.

The gonidia also have grown. They have begun to divide and form daughter colonies, which are visible around the edges. ▸

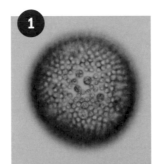

◂ This *Volvox* colony has been magnified 400 times.

▾ This *Volvox* colony, magnified 400 times, has just emerged from the parent colony.

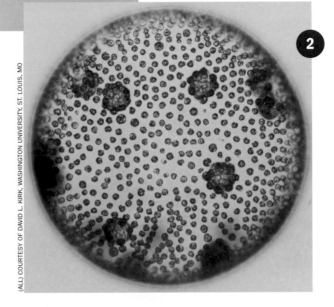

(ALL) COURTESY OF DAVID L. KIRK, WASHINGTON UNIVERSITY, ST. LOUIS, MO

Volvox Up Close

These two images show an adult *Volvox* colony in more detail. In this image, you can see gonidia in the process of dividing.

In the image at left, you can see the two hairlike lines attached to each cell. They are the flagella.

Older Adult

At three days, the colony has grown even more. In **PHOTO 3**, the daughter colonies are getting ready to leave the parent colony and live on their own.

In some of the colonies, you can see the gonidia that will produce the next generation of *Volvox*.

The parent cells of the sphere are now much smaller. The new cells used their contents as food.

Emerging

Most of the daughter colonies have now escaped through an opening in the adult colony. You can see in **PHOTO 4** that one new colony is moving out.

After all the young have left, the adult colony will fall apart. Its remaining contents will become food for the offspring. The daughter colonies will then repeat this cycle.

The next time you see green pond water, think about *Volvox*. Perhaps you should conduct your own investigation into the microscopic creatures living in a lake or pond near you. ■

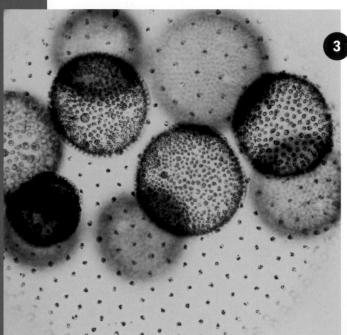

3

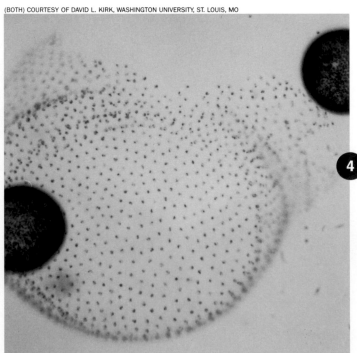

4

Vinegar Eelworm

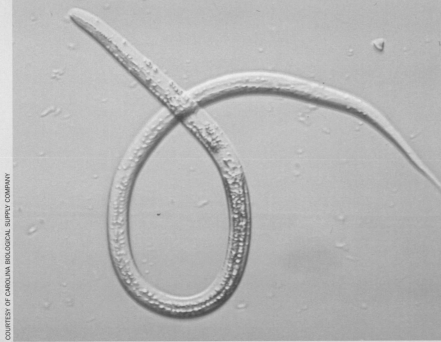

COURTESY OF CAROLINA BIOLOGICAL SUPPLY COMPANY

This is what a vinegar eelworm looks like under a light microscope. This creature is almost transparent. Do you see the shadowy shapes inside of the vinegar eelworm? Those are its organs.

HOW DID THE VINEGAR EELWORM GET ITS NAME? IT LOOKS SOMEWHAT LIKE AN EEL, BUT IT'S MUCH, MUCH SMALLER. AND IT DOESN'T LIVE IN A RIVER OR AN OCEAN. IT'S CALLED A VINEGAR EELWORM BECAUSE OF THE PLACE WHERE IT DOES LIVE. YOU GUESSED IT— IN VINEGAR!

THIS WORM DOESN'T LIVE IN THE KIND OF VINEGAR YOU BUY IN THE SUPERMARKET.

THAT VINEGAR IS PASTEURIZED. IT HAS UNDERGONE A HEATING PROCESS THAT KILLS THE MICROORGANISMS LIVING IN IT THAT MIGHT BE HARMFUL TO PEOPLE. ▶

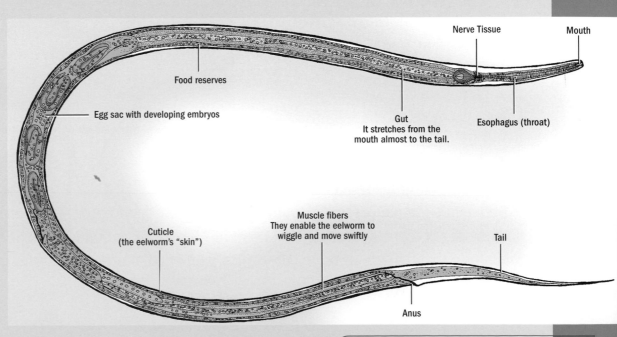

Nerve Tissue

Mouth

Food reserves

Egg sac with developing embryos

Gut
It stretches from the mouth almost to the tail.

Esophagus (throat)

Cuticle
(the eelworm's "skin")

Muscle fibers
They enable the eelworm to wiggle and move swiftly

Tail

Anus

No, the vinegar eelworm thrives in vinegar that is full of microorganisms. So it's not surprising that vinegar eelworms can also be found in decaying fruit such as apples and pears. Although eelworms thrive in these environments, they are not parasites. Some people even culture eelworms to use as fish bait.

Under an SEM

The image below right shows how the vinegar eelworm's head looks under an SEM. Its head has been magnified 800 times. Some of the white specks on the eelworm are bacteria. The diagram at the upper right points out the important parts of the worm's head.

Six lips circle the mouth. The lips help suck in food. The eelworm feeds on microorganisms that live in vinegar or some decaying fruits.

The eelworm does not have eyes, but it does have other ways of sensing its surroundings. The structures that help it do this are called chemoreceptors. Some help the eelworm by leading it to chemicals that indicate food is near and away from chemicals that indicate an enemy is near.

Between each pair of lips is a small, round sensory receptor. This worm has six sensory receptors. Can you see them all? These receptors are sensitive to touch and taste. They help the eelworm sense what comes near its mouth.

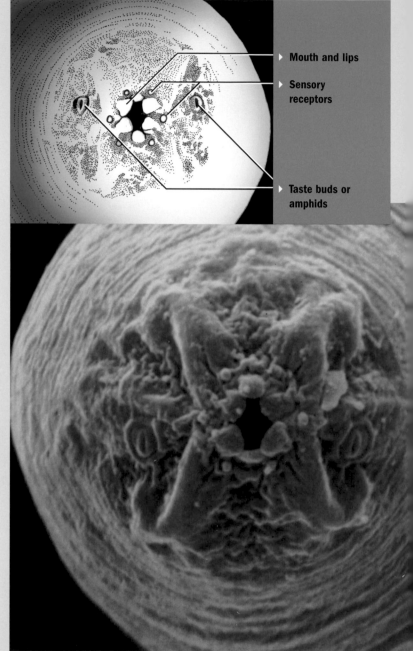

Compare the diagram of the vinegar eelworm's head, as seen directly below, with the photo below. Can you pick out some of the labeled organs in the photo?

Mouth and lips

Sensory receptors

Taste buds or amphids

A vinegar eelworm's head as seen under an SEM.

Two large receptors, called amphids, detect taste. You might think of these receptors as the eelworm's taste buds. Your taste buds are also chemoreceptors.

Under a Transmission Electron Microscope

While an SEM magnifies the outside of an organism, another kind of a microscope— a transmission electron microscope, or TEM—shows the inside of an organism. This TEM photo, at right, shows a cross-section of the eelworm at the base of its esophagus. The slice is magnified 3,000 times.

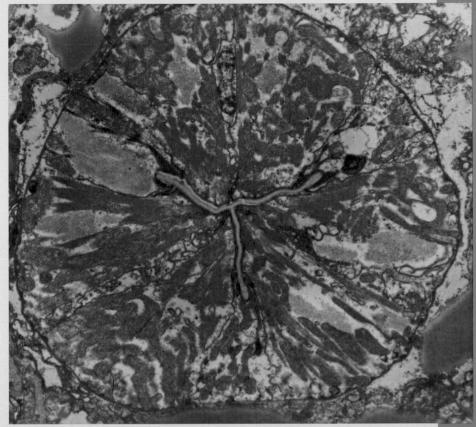

A slice of a vinegar eelworm as seen under a TEM

(BOTH) DUANE HOPE, NATIONAL MUSEUM OF NATURAL HISTORY, SMITHSONIAN INSTITUTION

Now you've seen a vinegar eelworm three ways: through a light microscope, an SEM, and a TEM. You've also seen a diagram of the organism and a close-up of its head.

By looking at all five images, what can you learn about this animal? How do all these images work together to give you a complete picture of the vinegar eelworm? ■

It's a Wormy World

Every time you walk in your back yard, you step on hundreds of thousands of relatives of the vinegar eelworm. They're known as threadworms, because they look like tiny pieces of thread. These worms are everywhere—in the soil, in oceans and rivers, on plants, and inside animals.

A threadworm is just one example of a very large group of worms called nematodes. There are more than 80,000 kinds of nematodes. Most are so small that you can't see them without the aid of a microscope.

Not all nematodes are microscopic in size. Some are quite large. One of these, the guinea worm, is a parasite. A parasite is an organism that feeds on another organism and contributes nothing to the survival of its host. The guinea worm can live under people's skin. It grows there and can get to be as long as 1 meter (about 3 feet).

Two other nematode parasites are quite common. Heartworm is one. It can harm your dog. Pinworm is a kind of parasite that people can get. It can cause an annoying rash.

Parasitic nematodes can be a danger to crops, too. They can cause plant diseases. Sometimes, nematodes feeding

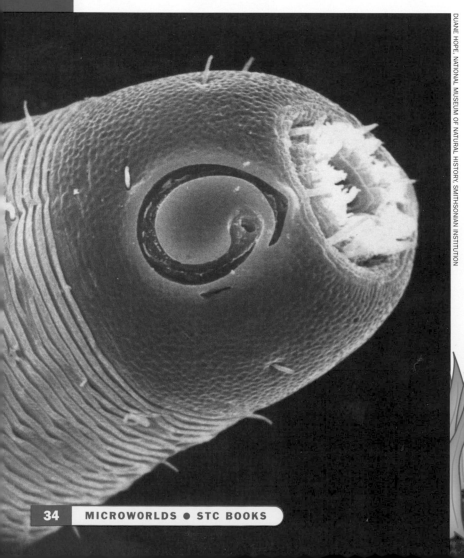

This is the head of a threadworm. It has been magnified 1,000 times.

underground prevent plants from absorbing water and nutrients through their root systems. Then the plants don't grow as well.

The largest known nematode is a parasite that grows inside a blue whale. Some of these worms can be 6.5 meters (about 21 feet) long.

What Do Threadworms Look Like?

All threadworms have the same simple shape. Like the vinegar eelworm, they are long and slender and do not have arms or legs. If you examine them closely under a high-powered microscope, you can see some interesting features.

Look back at the head of the threadworm on page 34. The bristly part at the tip of the head is the mouth. This particular threadworm has a series of grooves on the side of its head. Not all threadworms have these grooves. These grooves, called amphids, can detect chemicals in the environment. Chemical sensing is a job your nose, tongue, and skin all do for you.

Dinner Time

These pictures show the mouths of two threadworms. Look at each one closely. What do you think each one eats? ▸

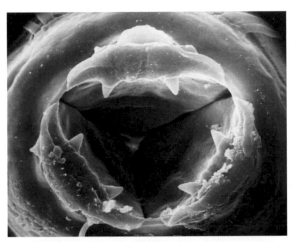

This image is of the mouth of a threadworm called *Enoplus*. It was taken through an SEM and magnified 1,500 times.

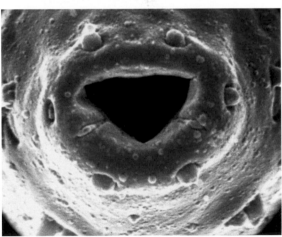

This is an SEM image of the mouth of *Phanoderma*. It has been magnified 3,000 times.

What do you think the threadworm with the large teeth eats? If you said meat, you're right. It is a predator—a creature that gets its food mainly from killing and eating other animals. When this type of threadworm is around, other tiny creatures need to look out!

The one with the smaller mouth feeds on bacteria, fungi, and organisms in the soil.

Nematodes are small but mighty. Some species can harm other animals and plant life. And they're survivors—they have a great ability to adapt to changes in their environment.

In fact, it has been said that if you were looking at a forest and could see nothing but the nematodes, you would be able to see an outline of almost every living thing in the forest. That's because just about all wild organisms have nematodes growing in them. So it's no surprise that nematodes are one of the most abundant types of animal life on Earth. ■

Smile
AND MEET SOME
Bacteria

SMILE AT YOURSELF IN THE MIRROR. You'll see shiny teeth and a happy face. You won't see bacteria, but they're there, too—all over your smile. Even after you've brushed your teeth and washed your face, plenty of bacteria remain.

And that's just the start. Bacteria are on your skin and hair and in your nose, throat, and intestines. Thanks to you, millions of bacteria have homes.

But don't start considering yourself special. You're not the only place where bacteria live. These microbes are everywhere: on the ground, in the air, in water, and inside plants. They are also found in extreme environments—in the frozen Arctic, in boiling springs, in the

All human beings—even you—are covered with bacteria.

COURTESY OF COLGATE-PALMOLIVE

air, at the bottom of the ocean, and deep in the ground.

Some bacteria are helpful. Bacteria that live near plant roots produce vitamins that help plants grow. Still other bacteria break down dead plants and animals so other organisms can reuse those chemicals.

Other bacteria can be harmful. *Streptococcus* gives you strep throat, a nasty infection. Another bacterium to avoid is *Salmonella*. *Salmonella* can be found in raw eggs and chicken. If you eat those foods when they are not completely cooked, you eat live *Salmonella*, too. Then you can get really sick.

Both helpful and harmful bacteria share many characteristics. Read on to learn more about them. ▸

What Do Bacteria Look Like?

There are more than 10,000 kinds of bacteria. But all of them look more or less like one of the three types of bacteria in the pictures below. In other words, nearly every bacterium is shaped like a ball, a spiral, or a rod. Of course, you can't see the shape of the bacteria unless you look at them through a powerful microscope. Bacteria are so small that thousands can fit on the head of a pin.

▼ **Spiral bacteria magnified 78,000 times**

▼ **Ball-shaped bacteria, or cocci, magnified 34,000 times**

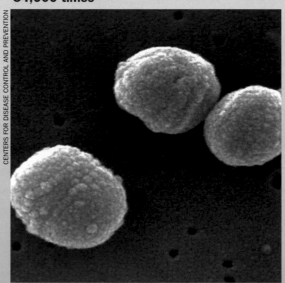

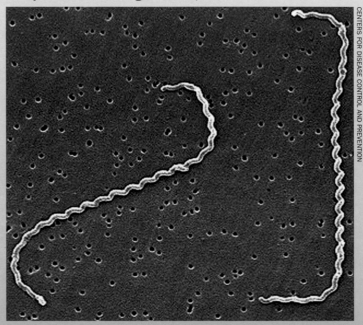

CENTERS FOR DISEASE CONTROL AND PREVENTION

CENTERS FOR DISEASE CONTROL AND PREVENTION

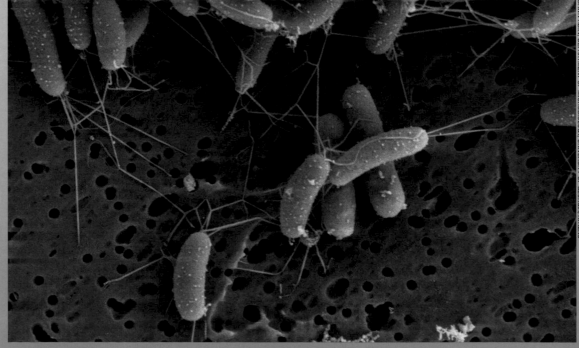

▶ **Rod-shaped bacteria, magnified 21,000 times. Can you see the bacteria's flagella?**

DAWN ADIN, DEPARTMENT OF MICROBIOLOGY, UNIVERSITY OF GEORGIA, ATHENS

How Do Bacteria Spend Their Time?

You'll never find a lone bacterium. That's why we usually see the word written in its plural form—bacteria. Bacteria live in large groups. They hang around others like themselves, breathing, eating, and producing more bacteria. They reproduce quickly. Within hours, a few bacteria can become a group with more individuals than the human population of New York City. (That's more than 8 million people!) But bacteria reproduce that rapidly only under certain conditions. Most of the time, they reproduce slowly.

Eating and Breathing

Bacteria absorb nutrients directly from their environment, much as a paper towel soaks up liquid. Some feed on minerals, while others use the sun's energy to make their own food.

Some kinds of bacteria don't need oxygen. Instead, they "breathe" other chemicals, such as nitrites or sulfates. These kinds of bacteria live where there is little or no oxygen: underground and at the bottom of lakes.

Moving

Some bacteria have thin whiplike structures called flagella. The flagella enable the bacteria to move. Among the speediest bacteria are the *Spirilla*. They are equipped with one or more flagella. The flagella are arranged in clumps or spread all over the body. Many kinds of cocci and bacilli have no flagella, and lack the ability to move.

These bacteria have whiplike flagella. They use these flagella to move around.

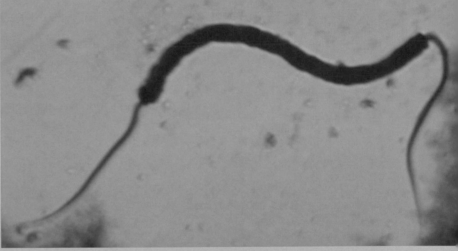

COURTESY OF CAROLINA BIOLOGICAL SUPPLY COMPANY

Every day, we come in contact with at least some bacteria. Each day, we wash them off our faces or brush them off our teeth, but we can't get rid of them. That's okay. They can help our environment in many ways.

But watch out for the harmful ones. They can be dangerous. So listen to grown-ups, and always wash your hands! ■

You Are What You *Eat*

There is a popular saying, "You are what you eat." Is this true? Read this colorful tale about a microbe and a bird that feeds upside down. Then decide for yourself.

Stretching down most of the length of East Africa is a giant valley. It is called the African Rift Valley. This valley has formed over millions of years along a line where the continent of Africa is splitting apart. The valley is dotted by volcanoes and steaming hot springs. The valley contains many lakes—big and small.

Some of the lakes of the African Rift Valley support a wide variety of organisms. But other lakes there are too salty to support much life. In fact, these lakes are much saltier than the sea. Few fish or plants can survive in their waters. While it is difficult for most forms of life to survive in these salty lakes, they do support a few hardy organisms. These species have adapted to these extreme conditions.

From space, these salty lakes often look pink. Why not green or blue, like other lakes?

The African Rift Valley stretches through the tropics of East Africa. It has many hot springs and volcanoes.

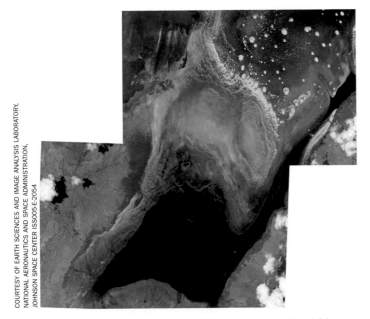

COURTESY OF EARTH SCIENCES AND IMAGE ANALYSIS LABORATORY,
NATIONAL AERONAUTICS AND SPACE ADMINISTRATION,
JOHNSON SPACE CENTER ISS005-E-2054

Lake Natron, one of the lakes of the African Rift Valley, has pink water. Why isn't it green or blue?

Shocking Pink

In the salty water lives a microbe called *Spirulina*. *Spirulina* is very hardy. Thousands can live in a spoonful of the salty lake water. *Spirulina* contains pigments that help it make food from sunlight and simple chemicals. One of these pigments is green. This gives *Spirulina* its green color. Another is reddish-orange. This reddish-orange substance is called carotene. Where else do you think carotene can be found?

Strange things happen to some organisms that eat *Spirulina*. They turn pink! For example, take the tiny pink

Spirulina is an example of a group of organisms known as cyanobacteria. Although it is green, it also contains an orange pigment called carotene.

brine shrimp. They are almost colorless until they feed on *Spirulina*. Where do you think the pink color comes from? The carotene in their food has made them change color. In fact, these shrimp are found in such large numbers in certain lakes of the Rift Valley that they turn the water pink.

Flamingos Have Different Tastes

But what about bigger animals that live on these lakes? For example, ▸

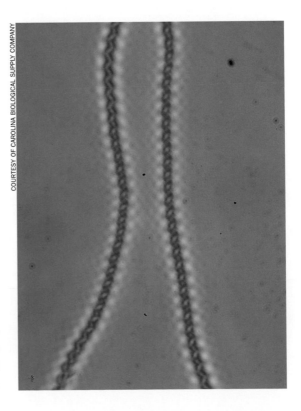

COURTESY OF CAROLINA BIOLOGICAL SUPPLY COMPANY

some lakes support huge flocks of flamingos. What color are they? And why?

To answer these questions, you first need to know about how these birds eat. If you watch any flamingo feed, you will see that it turns its head upside down and puts its beak into the water. The flamingo then pumps water in and out of its beak. It is using its beak to strain small organisms out of the water. Fine hairs on its beak catch such organisms in the water. Among them are a lot of shrimp.

In Africa, there are two species of flamingo. One, the Lesser Flamingo, feeds off *Spirulina*. The more *Spirulina* a Lesser Flamingo eats, the fatter—and pinker—it becomes. The bigger flamingo species, called the Greater Flamingo, doesn't eat *Spirulina* directly. Instead, it filters out and eats the brine shrimp that eat the *Spirulina*. As a result, the Greater Flamingo is not quite so pink.

COURTESY OF DAVID MARSLAND

There are two types of flamingos—the Lesser and the Greater. The Lesser Flamingo filters *Spirulina* from the water. The Greater Flamingo filters out the tiny brine shrimp that eat *Spirulina*.

Staying Pink in the Zoo

How do we know that flamingo feathers aren't naturally pink in color? When flamingos don't eat food with *Spirulina*—that is, food with carotene—they are white.

This is a problem for zoos. Flamingos are famous for being pink. Zoo visitors prefer pink to white flamingos. It is difficult for zoos to provide pink brine shrimps to feed their flocks. But zookeepers have solved this problem. They feed the flamingos other foods with lots of carotene in them—like carrots.

Perhaps flamingos, like people, are not exactly what they eat, but these birds certainly display one characteristic of their food. That characteristic makes flocks of hundreds of thousands of *pink* flamingos one of the greatest natural wonders of the African Rift Valley. ∎

Microorganisms Up Close

THAT'S A FACT! Almost all bacteria are shaped like a ball, a spiral, or a rod. Some bacteria have flagella, whiplike structures that enable the bacteria to move.

THAT'S EASY! Why are pink flamingos pink? What do microorganisms have to do with it?

WHAT DO YOU THINK? How are bacteria and nematodes similar? How are they different? Are they helpful, harmful—or both?

Part 3

Microorganisms and Microscopes in Our Lives

Microorganisms affect us all in more ways than you can imagine. For example, did you know that microorganisms are used to make vaccines? And that some bacteria can help make food taste better? The stories discuss these and other ways that microorganisms and microscopes are part of our lives.

Both of these scientists made important contributions to our understanding of the world. What characteristics do their experiments share?

LIBRARY OF CONGRESS, PRINTS & PHOTOGRAPHS DIVISION, LC-USZ62-3499

You'll find the following stories in this section:
- Good Guys, Bad Guys
- The Maggots' Tale
- How Pasteur Discovered a Vaccine
- Vaccination
- Feather Detectives

By the time you've read the stories in this section, you will think about microworlds in a whole new way.

Good Guys,

DO YOU KNOW HOW THESE FOODS ARE MADE?

H ow do you turn milk into yogurt? You put some bacteria to work. Many kinds of microbes can make things ferment. Fermentation is the chemical process during which some microbes break down their food. This process releases energy and some waste products.

One kind of bacterium that causes fermentation is naturally present in cows' milk. Under the right conditions —that is, when no oxygen is present— these bacteria grow and feed on the sugar in milk, turning the milk into yogurt. As these bacteria feed on the sugar, they turn it into other chemicals. These chemicals make plain yogurt taste sour instead of sweet and give the yogurt its characteristic smell. The bacterium that "makes" yogurt is called *Lactobacillus acidophilus.*

Other fermenting bacteria change cucumbers to pickles and cabbage to sauerkraut.

Still other microbes change soybeans into soy sauce. People in cultures around the world have discovered the value of putting bacteria to work!

What do these foods have in common?

Without bacteria, we would not have yogurt, which a lot of people really enjoy.

Grown in a Lab

In earlier days, people just let these bacteria mixtures work on their own. Today, food companies grow specific bacteria in a lab and add them directly to the foods they want to ferment.

The next time you eat some yogurt, read the package. It should say, "Contains active yogurt cultures" or "Contains *L. acidophilus.*" That label means "Fermenting bacteria at work." Don't worry, though. These bacteria are "good guys."

Bad Guys

Bacteria as Bad Guys

One bacterium that is very dangerous is called *Mycobacterium tuberculosis*. It can cause a serious disease called tuberculosis, or TB. This bacterium can live and grow only inside living tissues—like those in your body. *M. tuberculosis* needs oxygen, so the lung is an ideal place for these bacteria to live.

How do they get there? If an infected person coughs, the surrounding air can become contaminated with bacteria. Another person breathes in these bacteria, which settle into the new person's lungs.

Until the middle of the 20th century, TB was a major killer in the United States. Although the disease is less common today, new cases are still being reported. But now we have ways to protect ourselves from this deadly bacterium. We have vaccines that put our bodies on the alert for certain types of bacteria. The vaccine is made of a non-disease-causing form of the bacterium. That allows our bodies to make TB-fighting antibodies.

Another kind of bacterium, although closely related to the "good guy" fermenters, can make you very sick. It's *Clostridium botulinum*. This bacterium causes a kind of food poisoning called botulism. *Clostridium* grows only where there is no oxygen—for example, inside a can of food that has been improperly preserved. As these bacteria grow, they produce poisons that can be dangerous. These poisons can cause breathing difficulties, muscle paralysis, or death.

Today, however, canning companies have developed excellent sanitation procedures. They use plenty of heat when preparing their cans. That heat kills harmful bacteria. Still, you should never eat food from a bulging can or one with dents at its seams. These are possible signals of the presence of harmful bacteria.

When it comes to the "bad" bacteria, it's important to take precautions—don't eat improperly preserved food, and get all the vaccinations you need to protect yourself against infectious diseases. But remember, some bacteria can be good guys, too. After all, if you didn't have a pickle to go with that cheeseburger, life would be far less tasty! ■

Thanks to vaccines, kids throughout the world are protected from the bacteria that cause TB. These kids were among the first to be vaccinated.

The Maggots'

WHEN YOU LOOK AT PLANTS GROWING IN A GARDEN, YOU KNOW THAT THEY CAME FROM OTHER PLANTS. YOU ALSO KNOW THAT PUPPIES COME FROM DOGS AND KITTENS FROM CATS. BELIEVE IT OR NOT, PEOPLE DIDN'T ALWAYS KNOW THAT. BACK IN THE 1600S, PEOPLE THOUGHT THAT LIVING THINGS COULD COME FROM NONLIVING THINGS. FOR EXAMPLE, IF THEY SAW FROGS HOPPING AROUND A POND, THEY THOUGHT THAT THE FROGS CAME FROM MUD IN THE POND. THIS IDEA IS CALLED SPONTANEOUS GENERATION.

It took scientists to change such ideas. Francesco Redi, an Italian physician, developed a series of experiments to challenge this way of thinking. He did this work in the 1600s. Even though he didn't use microscopic creatures in his work, he did make a strong case that all living things developed from other organisms like themselves. That was his hypothesis. He then developed a series of experiments to test his hypothesis.

Redi was among the first scientists to challenge the idea of spontaneous generation.

Tale

Redi's Experiment

Redi noticed that maggots, white, wormlike fly larvae, frequently appeared in meat. Remember, he lived before people had refrigerators. Meat was often left uncovered, at room temperature.

Redi didn't want maggots on his meat. You can't blame him for that.

HERE'S HOW REDI SET UP HIS EXPERIMENT.

FIRST, he cooked some raw meat and then divided it into three jars.

According to the idea of spontaneous generation, the maggots must have come from the meat. But Redi didn't believe that was true. He thought that maggots were the offspring of flies that had been attracted to the meat. He speculated that the flies had feasted on the meat, then laid their eggs on it before they flew away.

- He sealed Jar 1 with parchment, or animal skin.
- He covered Jar 2 with sheer, clean cloth.
- He left Jar 3 uncovered. ▸

Redi covered the first jar with parchment, or animal skin.

This cloth was not as thick as the parchment. But it still protected the meat from flies.

The meat in this jar is not protected at all.

The Predictions

Redi made the following predictions:

1. Flies won't be able to smell the meat in Jar 1. There will be no flies—and no maggots—in Jar 1.

2. The odor of the meat will attract flies to Jar 2, but the cloth will prevent them from entering it. As a result, there will be no maggots on this meat.

3. Flies will enter Jar 3. They will lay their eggs on the meat in the jar. When the eggs hatch, the maggots will emerge.

The Results

Redi watched the three jars for several weeks. What do you think he saw? Take a minute to think about what happened. You may want to write down your ideas on a sheet of paper.

Here are the results of his experiment.

1. The flies didn't go near Jar 1. Even after several weeks, there were no maggots on the meat.

No flies here!

2. Many flies were attracted to Jar 2. They landed on the cloth and walked around. But the flies never got inside. They never touched the meat.

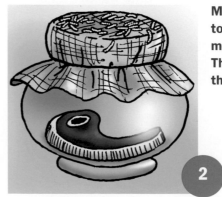

Maggots never touched the meat in Jar 2. The cloth kept them out.

Several days later, there still were no maggots in the meat. But there were maggots on the cloth covering the jar.

3. Dozens of flies landed on the meat in Jar 3, the uncovered jar. The flies spent some time there. Then they flew away. After several weeks, the meat in Jar 3 was full of maggots.

3

This meat was covered with maggots. Not very appetizing—for humans, that is!

To make sure his results were reliable, Redi repeated the experiment many times. He always got the same results. When he thought he had enough evidence, he put the ideas together.

Here are his conclusions:

1. The maggots came from eggs that the flies laid. Fly eggs are so tiny that they can barely be seen with the naked eye. People didn't realize that the specks they often saw on meat were fly eggs.

2. Living things—regardless of their size—come only from other living things. They do not appear spontaneously, as if by magic. The maggots are larvae that become adult flies.

Redi's conclusion applies to all organisms. All living things—from the tiniest bacteria to human beings—come from other living things like themselves. This idea sounds obvious to us, but it was a landmark discovery.

Redi's conclusions changed the way people looked at all the creatures that inhabit our world, including those maggots. ■

How Pasteur Discovered a Vaccine

Louis Pasteur

IT WAS 1879. FARMERS IN FRANCE WERE BRINGING ALARMING NEWS TO A FAMOUS SCIENTIST LIVING NEARBY. "OUR CHICKENS ARE DYING OF CHOLERA. WE CAN'T AFFORD TO LOSE ALL OUR CHICKENS. CAN YOU HELP US FIGURE OUT WHICH GERM IS RESPONSIBLE?"

The scientist was Louis Pasteur. He was known for discovering that certain germs are the cause of many diseases. Pasteur also knew of the work of a scientist named Edward Jenner. Jenner had developed a vaccine for another nasty disease—smallpox. The only problem was that Pasteur didn't know how Jenner had made his vaccine. He would have to figure that out.

If Pasteur had been faced with this problem 20 years earlier, he would have started working by himself. But at this point in his career, Pasteur had also learned an important lesson: Scientists can make more progress by working with other scientists. He decided to collaborate with a scientist named Charles Chamberland.

First Pasteur created a mixture full of cholera germs.

Pasteur then gave the chickens a small shot of cholera mixture to test his hypothesis that germs cause disease.

The Search for the Germ

THE FIRST STEP FOR PASTEUR AND CHAMBERLAND was to find the germ that causes cholera. Pasteur hypothesized that diseased chickens would have a germ that healthy chickens would not. He looked for cholera-causing germs in the blood of the diseased chickens. Using blood from chickens that had died of cholera, he developed a mixture of cholera germs that he would use for his investigations.

NEXT, PASTEUR AND CHAMBERLAND TESTED THEIR HYPOTHESIS that the germs cause the disease by giving some healthy chickens a small shot of the cholera mixture. What result would you expect if the hypothesis was correct? What would you expect to see if Pasteur's hypothesis was wrong?

As you may have figured out, all the chickens died. This means that Pasteur and Chamberland's hypothesis was correct: Germs had caused the chickens to get sick and die. ▶

Pasteur was not surprised by the results of his experiment.

Experiments Put on Hold

In the middle of his investigation, Pasteur was called away from his laboratory for several weeks. He left the cholera mixture on his lab table.

Nobody touched the cholera mixture for several weeks.

When he returned home, he went back to his research. He decided to try the experiment again. He gave a new group of healthy chickens shots from the cholera mixture that had been sitting on the lab table.

These chickens didn't die. They got sick, but all the chickens in this group survived.

Pasteur gave a healthy chicken a shot from the weakened cholera mixture.

Making Progress

Pasteur thought about these results. Then he had an idea. Maybe the chickens in the second group didn't die because the cholera germs became weaker as they got older.

Pasteur and his team then thought about what would happen if he made a new batch of the cholera mixture and gave it to another group of chickens. Would they live or die?

Pasteur made a strong batch of the cholera mixture. He gave a third group of healthy chickens shots from this new batch. While he was at it, he also gave a shot of the new, strong mixture to the chickens in the second group, which had survived the injection of the cholera mixture that had grown weaker.

Getting Results and Drawing Conclusions

The next morning, Pasteur returned to his lab. What do you think he found? What happened to the second group? What about the third?

Here are the results of the experiment:

The chickens in the second group were fine. All the chickens in the third group were dead. Just like the chickens in the first group, they did not survive an injection of fresh germs.

Pasteur believed that the second group of chickens had used the weakened mixture of cholera germs to build up a defense against the germs in the new, strong mixture. Pasteur and his team had just discovered a vaccine against

cholera. Pasteur next went on to work on a vaccine for rabies.

Vaccines were a major step forward for medical science. Now, in addition to treating diseases, doctors could also focus on preventing them. Thanks to vaccines, outbreaks of many bacterial and viral diseases—including cholera, typhoid fever, polio, chickenpox, and mumps—can be prevented.

Healthy chickens at last! What a breakthrough!

cholera. A vaccine is a substance that contains weakened or killed microbes. When the chickens were injected with the mixture of weak cholera germs, their bodies' defenses were alerted to this germ. They used it to build antibodies to cholera. When they were later exposed to young, deadly cholera germs, the antibodies fought back right away.

Building on the work of Jenner, Pasteur and Chamberland had discovered a vaccine for another disease,

Pasteur was a creative and careful scientist. His contribution to the concept of vaccines was a major step in medical science. Although Pasteur and his team knew that the vaccine worked, they didn't understand how. That discovery would come much later. ■

Vaccination

Vaccination

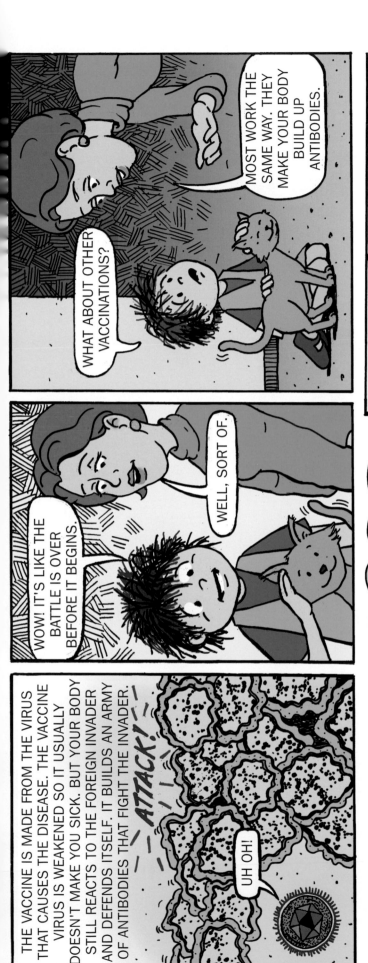

Feather Detectives

Carla Dove and Marcy Heacker are partners in crime at the Smithsonian
Institution's National Museum of Natural History.

The $20 Million Flock

Imagine you are an Air Force pilot flying a fighter jet at almost the speed of sound. Almost anything that hits your plane—including a flock of birds—could cause major damage. It doesn't take much to put a plane out of action.

On March 21, 2001, a flock of birds hit an F-16 at close to 500 meters (1640 feet) over Florida. The birds put a hole in a fuel tank, forcing the plane to make an emergency landing. Right after landing, the plane caught fire. Fortunately, no one was hurt, but the cost to the Air Force was almost $20 million.

Hitting a plane head-on is not the only way that birds can interfere with planes. Sometimes a bird can be sucked into a jet engine. That's bad news for the bird, and it's not good for the plane either. The giant fans that suck air through the engine could be severely damaged.

There are about 9,000 species, or kinds, of birds, and each species behaves differently. Knowing how birds behave can help reduce the chance of bird-plane collisions.

CARLA DOVE AND MARCY HEACKER, NATIONAL MUSEUM OF NATURAL HISTORY, SMITHSONIAN INSTITUTION

Scientists Get Involved

This is where scientists step in. Scientific studies of bird behavior provide one side of the bird strike-prevention story. The other involves identifying birds that strike the planes. Put this information into a large computer file, or database, and you have a useful tool for determining the likelihood that certain birds will hit planes.

The problem with identifying birds that have hit planes is that often not much is left of the birds. What remains are the feathers. To figure out which feathers belong to which birds, call on Carla Dove and Marcy Heacker, feather detectives at the National Museum of Natural History, part of the Smithsonian Institution in Washington, D.C.

Solving the Mystery, One Feather at a Time

The first step for Carla and Marcy is to collect "feather evidence" from the scene of the strike. The more feathers, the better. When the feathers arrive at the lab, they are washed and dried. Sometimes it's possible to identify the bird species from the cleaned feathers. Carla and Marcy use the Smithsonian's huge collection of bird feathers to help them. ▸

BARBULES

BARBS

(ALL) CARLA DOVE AND MARCY HEACKER, NATIONAL MUSEUM OF NATURAL HISTORY, SMITHSONIAN INSTITUTION

◀ Feathers like this one may be found in or near a plane after a bird strike.

▼ After each feather arrives in the lab, it is washed in a mild, soapy solution. Washing also helps the feather regain its natural shape.

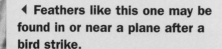

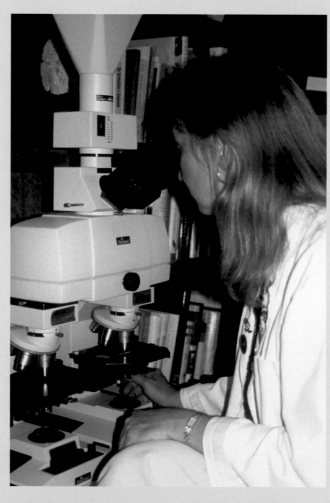

▲ Carla looks at a feather under a microscope, gaining valuable information about its shape and structure.

But the problem with identifying birds just by studying the feathers with your eyes is that many feathers look alike. For example, lots of bird feathers are brown. So when Carla and Marcy need more information, they turn to a microscope.

Look at any bird feather like the one at the top of the page and you will see that it consists of a shaft with lots of barbs, or individual feather strands, attached to it. At the base of the feather are the fluffy, downy barbs. Scientists like Carla and Marcy use these barbs to help identify

Here are turkey and white-fronted goose feather barbs magnified 500 times. The feathers on the left are goose feathers. The barbules are triangular. The turkey feathers, below, have ring shaped barbules. It's easy to tell them apart with a microscope.

groups of birds. Under the microscope, more structures are revealed. Then it is possible to see the barbules, tiny structures where each feather cell links to another.

Different bird species have different barb and barbule structures. Barbules may have different features such as hooks, prongs, and pigments, or colors. By observing carefully and comparing the samples with slides of other bird feathers, scientists can identify the species from which the feather came.

Combining Information

Like all good detective work, the trick is to put all the clues together. Information from observing the feathers, viewing them under the microscope, and noting the location of the bird strike all provide clues. But what happens once you've identified the bird? How is this information useful? And why bother collecting it?

There are several good reasons to collect such information. Stored in computer databases, the information can be used to prevent bird strikes from happening in the future. Once scientists know which birds are likely to strike in what area, they can develop strategies to keep those birds away.

Another good use of data on bird strikes is for improving the design of aircraft. Engineers have used this information to improve the design of parts of the F-16 and commercial aircraft so they do not sustain damage so easily when birds do hit them.

The more data the feather detectives can provide, the safer flying becomes—for birds, for pilots, for planes, and for us. ■

(BOTH) ROXIE LAYBOURNE, NATIONAL MUSEUM OF NATURAL HISTORY, SMITHSONIAN INSTITUTION

Microorganisms and Microscopes in Our Lives

THAT'S A FACT!   Louis Pasteur was a pioneer in the invention of vaccines, but even he didn't understand how they worked. That would take many more years of scientific investigation.

I KNOW THAT!   Why is it important to study feather evidence under a microscope?

WHAT DO YOU THINK?   Now that you've read the stories in this section, do you know how Pasteur and Redi's experiments were similar? What elements do all scientific investigations have in common?

Glossary

ALGA: *(Plural: Algae)* An organism that shares many qualities with plants, including the ability to make its own food.

ANTIBODY: A chemical, produced by cells in the immune system, that destroys a specific kind of microbe.

BACTERIUM: A tiny, one-celled organism.

CELL: The smallest organized unit of life.

CHLOROPHYLL: A green pigment found in the leaves of plants and in some algae; this pigment absorbs the light energy from the sun that plants need to make their own food.

DATABASE: An electronic file that stores key information about a certain topic; many people can use the file. It is an effective way to pool scientific knowledge.

FERMENTATION: A chemical process in which an organic molecule splits into simpler substances; often the agent for change is bacteria digestion. This process takes place without the presence of oxygen.

FLAGELLA: Whiplike structures that enable some organisms, such as bacteria, to move.

HYPOTHESIS: A possible explanation for a set of observations or answers to a given scientific question; this explanation must be testable.

MICROBE: A particular kind of microorganism. Often refers to those that cause disease.

MICROORGANISM: A living thing that is so small that it can be seen clearly only through a microscope.

MICROSCOPE: A tool designed to magnify objects and organisms that are too small to be seen with the eyes alone.

NEMATODE: Any of a large group of long, thin worms, many of which are microscopic; some are parasites.

PARASITE: An organism that usually lives on or inside another organism; the parasite is dependent on the host organism but makes no contribution toward sustaining it. It is harmful to the host.

PASTEURIZATION: A heating process that kills microorganisms living in liquids such as vinegar.

PREDATOR: An animal that hunts and kills other animals for food and has adaptations that help it capture its prey.

PROTIST: A member of a diverse group of organisms that can resemble either plants or animals. All protists do share one characteristic—they live in moist places.

SCANNING ELECTRON MICROSCOPE (SEM): A powerful microscope that uses an electron beam to help view the surface of very tiny objects.

TRANSMISSION ELECTRON MICROSCOPE (TEM): A microscope that reveals the inside of a tiny object by passing electrons through a thin slice of it.

VACCINATION: A preventive form of medicine that is made up of weakened germs of particular microbes, such as those that cause cholera, rabies, or chickenpox.

VOLVOX: A kind of protist that is made up of one cell; *Volvox* live in colonies made up of as many as 50,000 cells.

photo credits